THE HEART AND SOUL OF THE DOMINICAN REPUBLIC

An American's View of His New Country

Robert S. Matthews

authorHOUSE®

AuthorHouse™
1663 Liberty Drive, Suite 200
Bloomington, IN 47403
www.authorhouse.com
Phone: 1-800-839-8640

First published by AuthorHouse 11/28/2007

ISBN: 978-1-4343-2741-3 (sc)

Library of Congress Control Number: 2007905639

Printed in the United States of America
Bloomington, Indiana

This book is printed on acid-free paper.

"The Heart and Soul of the Dominican Republic"

An American's View of His New Country

is enthusiastically dedicated to the compassionate, helpful, and gentle Dominican people who have lovingly and respectfully entered my life and adopted me as one of their family. A special praise and blessing on my Dominican wife, Providencia, my daughter, Alexandra, a dedicated mother to her three children and my grandchildren, Cherry, Edward, and Michael Liranzo.

CONTENTS

ARTICLE ONE

"Why The Dominican Republic Has Been A Tourist Attraction Since 1492"

On December 5, 1492, Don Christopher Columbus discovered the island of Hispañiola, now Haiti and the Dominican Republic. Though there were no luxurious hotels, swimming pools, and international and native restaurants along the beaches of the island, Admiral Columbus returned from Spain on three other voyages to visit his enchanting jewel of the West Indies. His "tourist" guides were the Taino Indians who called the island Bohio and Quisqueya that meant, "Mother of all lands." It was here in the Dominican Republic that Columbus loved the most and asked to be buried.

Why do so many vacationing Americans, Canadians, and Europeans insist on returning to the island where Columbus lived and loved the most? Why has Quisqueya or the Dominican Republic been one of the fastest growing vacation areas of the Caribbean? What are the main attractions for vacationing foreigners? What are some of the major concerns of tourists when they vacation outside their native country?

Answering the last question about the concerns of tourists when they vacation outside their country will also supply us with the information we need about the other questions.

My first concern when I go on a vacation out of my own homeland is the *attitude* of the native people toward foreign visitors, especially Americans. Is there an existing and perpetuating tranquility in the country that offers security to the unfamiliar traveler or visitor?

Tranquility prevails in the Dominican Republic. The peaceful, proud, and serene spirit of the Dominican people is the emotional catalyst that welcomes the world to its beaches, cities, and majestic mountains. The pacific inhabitants of this nation are proud of their culture, customs, and individual creativity that becomes gratuity to the world that will arrive for commercial, recreational, or residential interests. Here among the Dominican people is where I believe hospitality was invented. "Mi casa es tu casa" (my house is your house), is the phrase perhaps originally quoted in this gorgeous land. Tranquility is a daily Dominican product grown and cultivated in an enchanted environment.

My second concern and interest in locating a vacation area abroad is the existence of national and *environmental variety* that will attract my attention and prevent daily discontentment. Boredom prefers a changeless scene and unattractive surroundings. However, the variety of natural habitat and cultural activities flourish in the land Christopher Columbus loved the best. Thousands of North Americans and Europeans are returning year after year to vacation in the sanctuary of variety.

The geographical location and habitation of the Dominican Republic represents an environmental paradise for recreational adventurers. Though there is a terrestrial western border separating the country from Haiti, the Dominican Republic has 1,566 kilometers of coastline. The beaches consists of 35% of the coastline that is bordered on the north by the Atlantic Ocean, on the south by the Caribbean Sea, and on the east by the Mona Canal separating it from Puerto Rico ninety-one miles away.

There is also a variety of climate changes in a country where the average temperature is 77 degrees. The coastal areas are warm and typically tropical with temperatures ranging from 75 to 90 degrees Fahrenheit. However, a few hours away from the mild ocean climate is the Cordillera Central Massif, a mountain range of the central region of the country called Cibao. Here in Cibao the temperatures are known to have fallen as low as 32 degrees Fahrenheit in the winter months.

Variety of life is everywhere in the island that was discovered by Spain over 500 years ago. Spectacular scenery of the countryside can be seen along the 40 kilometers coco coast of fine white sand, crystalline waters, and endless coconut palms of the eastern beaches of Bavaro-Punta Cana-Cap Cana in La Altagracia. Perhaps you prefer to visit the 3,175 meters (over 10,000 feet) Mount Pico Duarte of Cibao, the highest elevation in the country. One cannot resist visiting the miles and miles of sugarcane fields of the southeast region to the amber coast of the Atlantic where Columbus made his maiden landing of the Santa Maria in 1492.

Variety in the Dominican Republic also comes in the form of historical and religious festivals and monumental architecture. The Basilica in the city of Higuey is a Roman Catholic Cathedral measuring 80 meters in height and can be seen from any point in the city and beyond. This huge Cathedral began to be built in 1954 during the administration of the fierce dictator, Trujillo, and finished in 1972 to honor La Virgen (Virgin Mary) De La Altagracia. The religious fiestas associated with the Basilica is the Fiesta of Toros from August 13th to the 17th in honor of Maria or Mary, and January 21st which is Higuey's largest and most well-known day in honor of the Virgen of Altagracia.

The oldest city in the Americas, Santo Domingo, contains a variety of colonial buildings from the early 1500's to the 17th century. Here in the capital city the visitor will be enchanted with the oldest European fort in the Americas, the oldest monastery, the first paved streets, and the oldest church building.

LA BASILICA IN THE CITY OF HIGUEY

Finally, variety exists in the country's greatest resource-its *people*. There is a racial mixture of European, African, and Indian blood in the families of the Dominican Republic. A typical Dominican family will have children who are dark-skinned, Indian brown, white, and many other possibilities in-between. This makes an interesting living-room portrait.

My third concern when I travel overseas for business or pleasure is *mobilization*. I need to know that there exists the convenience of transportation to and from the resort or wherever I may be visiting in the Dominican Republic.

Santo Domingo, the capital city, that is located on the south coast or the Caribbean Sea, is a transportation paradise affluently possessing a variety of mobilized activity within the city. The hub or central point for the departure and arrival of most minibuses, taxis, and other large buses is located where Avenida Duarte and 27 de Febrero come together just before crossing the Duarte bridge east toward the international airport. However, the traveler will have no problem finding the large city state buses called La Onza, minibuses, and taxis in any district of the capital city.

One of the most economical types of transportation within Santo Domingo on any major avenue are the private state-licensed cars called "derecho" or straight ahead. This ride will only cost the passenger about ten pesos if he or she is going straight ahead along the same street.

Minibuses or larger buses to any major town or city in the country are available from Santo Domingo. Once arriving at another city or the resorts near Boca Chica, Puerto Plata, or Bavaro-Punta Cana, for example, a traveler will also discover many forms of public and private transportation such as vans, taxis, tourist buses, and public minibuses.

A vacationer or traveler to the Dominican Republic will not feel he or she has been left stranded when arriving at the city's Las Americas International Airport, or at one of the airports near the attractive resorts such as La Romana and Bavaro-Punta Cana. There is an abundance of public transportation to and from these airports by means of buses, minibuses, vans, taxis, public cars, and as a last resort, the motorcycle taxis called motorconchos. Most of these airports will have twenty four hour taxis that are licensed with the state to operate and carry on business between the airports and the hotels along the beaches and in the cities.

My fourth major concern is *communication* or the need to be understood when seeking for solutions of problems, directions, or developing relationships.

One of the things that concern many visitors to the Dominican Republic is being able to communicate to the people and find their way around. Though the national language of the country is Spanish, there are trained native guides who have skills in English and the various languages of Europe. The hotels and public transportation also provide translator services in the language of their guests so that nobody will feel like they have been forgotten, lost, or abandoned on this beautiful island.

When a residential foreigner such as me has been living in the Dominican Republic, he soon discovers the availability of language institutes in every major city. It is heartwarming, therefore, to walk into one of these schools and hear students speak in my own language. Consequently, I was hired on the spot to teach English when the director heard my questions and responses to his students.

Last but not least is my interest in **relaxation** when I arrive at the original tourist attraction in the Caribbean. I can't prove it, but my guess is that Christopher Columbus and his men found time to relax on the sunny beaches when they arrived near what is now Puerto Plata. It was to be one of the most important voyages known to mankind. Now the news is out! The world is coming to relax from its stress and tiresome activities.

Relaxation comes in many forms in the Dominican Republic depending on the traveler or vacationer and the time the visitor will spend in this paradise. My favorite area for beach recreational activities is towards the land of the sunrise or the eastern region. Here is how I would spend a week of vacation in the Dominican Republic.

I prefer two or three days at the beach while staying in one of the spectacular hotels along the Coco Beach in Bavaro-Punta Cana. The next day I will explore the heights of Chavon and boat along its river not far from the Boca de Yuma. This area is just a few miles from the 500 year-old castle of Juan Ponce de Leon, the discover and first governor of Puerto Rico. The fourth day I would enjoy an excursion to Saona Island off the coast of Bayahibe near La Romana.

It is better in my opinion as a tourist and foreigner that you go in a group excursion from the hotel to all tourist locations in the capital city. The excursions are reasonable and they provide security, transportation, and tourist guides. Contact your favorite travel service or the representative in your hotel in Punta Cana/Bavaro for more information and professional service.

The fifth day will require a little more adventure due to the absence of a native guide. I will pay 50 pesos for transportation on a minibus from the hotel to the capital city bus station in the city of Higuey which should take only forty minutes. From Higuey I will pay about 120 pesos to ride on one of the large public buses for two and a half hours to Santo Domingo. From the Higuey bus station near Avenida Duarte and Parque Enriquillo I will pay about 60 pesos (about two dollars) for a taxi to take me to the city's Zona Colonial. I will pay another 50 to 100 pesos to a guide at the district to show me around at the oldest European settlement in the Americas. From there I may pay 100 pesos to another taxi and visit the Conde and its hundred's of stores where Independence was declared from Haiti on February 27, 1844. When finished at the Conde I will pay another 100 pesos for a taxi to bring me to the fabulous Faro A Colon Museum where the ashes of Columbus are guarded. This colossal museum has a room represented for each country in the western hemisphere. After spending at least an hour at the museum I will return me in a taxi to the Higuey bus station near Duarte where I can begin my trip back to Punta Cana.

When you know some Spanish and the capital city you can easily ask for a minibus that goes anywhere in the city and pay about ten pesos on each bus. This is exactly what I do now that I am acquainted with the transportation system in Santo Domingo. Though there will be a few occasions when it will be more convenient to take a taxi. You should always ask what the rate will be before you get in and go anywhere. This will prevent future misunderstandings between you and the driver.

When you discover the Dominican Republic, you will know why Christopher Columbus returned to this paradise again and again, and why it was the land he loved the most. Here in Quisqueya you have everything you need for your vacation and travel experiences to be successful. You will return again to love this land.

PUNTA CANA INTERNATIONAL AIRPORT

Article Two

*"The Tourist Most Talked About Unknown City In
The Dominican Republic"*

How does a small insignificant Caribbean city in the Dominican Republic become so well known among thousands of North American and European Tourists? Why is this tranquil notorious settlement known as La Otra Banda the one location that will be long remembered by the vacationing foreigners?

There are no gas stations, supermarkets, and beaches in this east-coast Dominican town thirty minutes from popular vacation resorts in Punta Cana. There are no cultural museums and statutes dedicated to Admiral Christopher Columbus. La Otra Banda is not known for any famous historical events on this island. The name of the city is not even on many of the country's national and local maps. Drivers of tourist buses dislike driving through the town because of the menacing speed bumps and a congested narrow main thoroughfare.

The growing city in the eastern province of La Altagracia is simply a passing-through point for tourists who are on their way to other recreational areas and the capital city, Santo Domingo. Most motorists and passengers are only enchanted by the hundreds of acres of sugarcane fields and farming country that surround the uncelebrated community of La Otra Banda.

However, the ten-minute excursion the tourist buses will make through my adopted Caribbean city will be long enough to engrave a permanent image in the minds of the traveling viewers. The foreign guests will never forget their short visit in my town. The city unintentionally provides free sidewalk entertainment while publicly marketing their products. The familiar daily objects of the city's patrons have become an unforgettable source of conversation among the foreign visitors.

I work almost daily in privately-owned tourist buses with Americans and Canadians visiting Punta Cana-Bavaro. My job is to provide information to the visitors while transporting them to their hotels on arrival, and to the airport when they are preparing to leave the country. Many of these tourists during their vacation will venture outside their hotels on organized tours to other interesting recreational and educational locations. I will often ask these departing foreigners in our journey to the airport if they remember visiting and passing through the city where I live while being transported on their tour.

"I live in La Otra Banda," I will boast. "Do you remember going through my community?" There are usually no responses, only perplexing looks as if to ask, "Where is La Otra Banda?" I will then explain, "La Otra banda is the small community about thirty minutes from here. You had to go through this town on the way to Santo Domingo. Now do you remember?" Once again I only receive confused blank stares from the red-skinned, sun-burnt vacationers. Finally, someone will have the courage to answer, "I don't believe we went through your city where you live."

I know they went through La Otra banda, but I won't challenge them on that. If you go to the capital city and other points West, you must travel through the town where I live. There are no other paved roads for the oversize tourist buses. There are no other reasons for vacationers to visit the city where I live except to get on the other side where the road leads to prominent recreational areas.

I won't give up seeking for the recognition I needed for the small city that has some of the most beautiful and grandeur houses among the Dominican residents of this province. I will be right up front with the tourists who are on my bus. I will be slightly embarrassed, but I will say it.

"I live in La Otra Banda, the city of the hanging meat. Did you see it?" I finally admitted. "Is that disgusting meat in La Otra Banda? Is that where you live?" someone asked. "The flies on that meat, oh....ugh," a woman commented in a choking whisper while several of the guests suddenly put their hands over their mouths. "Yes, I remember seeing all of that rotting meat in front of many stores. How can I ever forget that sight," another person added. "Ugh," several others groaned as they turned their faces away from me as if they were going to vomit. "Do people really eat that stuff hanging in the sun all day?" inquired an interested individual in the back of the bus. "Yes, but the people wash it first," I quickly responded in a friendly tone with a smile on my face.

The city I decided to live in while working in the Dominican Republic is recognized and remembered, unfortunately, for the hanging carcasses of cows, pigs, and goats. Nevertheless, the parade of the putrid fly infested meat from a dozen or so businesses along main street surprisingly has its own personality and charisma.

Many of the European visitors convince their chofers and tourist guides to make a thirty-minute pit stop at La Otra banda to take a closer look at the town's main attraction. The shy pale skin individuals approach the unfortunate naked victims with caution. They step lightly over the red streams of flowing blood that have already been dripping several hours from the raw meat.

Walking slightly bent over and with her head down, one of the European tourists gets a little too close, and within "striking" distance. She finally straightens herself up from the curious position and bumps her head into a glob of meat. With the early afternoon sun distorting her vision, the timid visitor peevishly glares at the object that has wetted the top of her head. "Ahh, help," she cries out as she quickly withdraws from the others. "A giant night crawler has attacked me and bit my head," she frantically yells. Some of her traveling companions begin to snicker and giggle while the frighten woman feverishly retreats to the tourist bus for "safety." The frightened foreigner's screaming voice was heard echoing the descriptive words of her attacker to the bus driver. "It has greasy gray-colored skin, an antenna, and several dead-like eyes."

From a distance and from a viewer distortion, spicy longaniza sausages have a similar shape to a giant worm. However, I've never known these hanging giant greasy sausages to bite and attack anyone. They just hang around all day in the hot Caribbean sun of my town until someone buys them for their afternoon or evening meal. These "violent worms" that prey on the heads of curious tourists are the only hanging meaty articles on public display that I eat.

There is rarely a dull moment in my adopted rustic town of La Otra Banda. It is the breeding ground for variety; hanging carcasses of pigs, cows, goats, and impressionable fly-covered seasoned sausages. When can we expect you for dinner? It doesn't matter! The hanging meat will always be here waiting for sightseers, and sometimes touchers of suspicious-looking sausages. You won't forget our entertainment, and it's free!

ARTICLE THREE

"How to Eliminate Beach Boredom If It Happens To You"

One of the worst things that can happen to an island vacationer is 'beach boredom' amidst magnificent hotel resorts and sparkling blue tropical waters. Imagine spending the remainder of your vacation in a romantic paradise such as the Dominican Republic and becoming bored of the Caribbean sun, the hot white beach sand, and body surfing. But it happens, and it can happen to you!

There are always some who will never experience boredom lying hours each day on the gorgeous beaches of the Dominican Republic. They can get body burned and tanned all day and every day of their Dominican vacation and remember it as the greatest thrill of their lives. However, there are those like myself who need to be involved in more daily variety as a tourist or visitor in a foreign country. This shall be called cultural exchange and contentment.

The many fine resorts in Punta Cana-Bavaro provide daily recreational attractions, international and native evening entertainment, and beach life activities that succumb to the pleasure and satisfaction of the European and North American tourists. Nevertheless, one's mind is curious for native cultural experiences just minutes away outside the environment of the hotel resort. Personal contentment and the elimination of beach boredom depends and thrives on the native Dominican environment and ethnic adventure.

First, ask yourself the following questions: Is it the modern-day conveniences and habitat of people that you prefer to visit? The capital city of Santo Domingo is a modern Caribbean metropolis with the contributions of fifteenth century historical colonial buildings, streets, and events of the Spanish Conquistadors. The daily shopping experiences of the crowded streets of downtown Santo Domingo is another experience you'll never forget. The all night restaurants featuring native or international cuisine with the music of merengue or bachata intensify the pleasure of the Dominican experience. The one-person small wooden hand push-carts selling fruits, sweets, juices, and sandwiches can be seen on every major street from dawn to the late hours of the evening. The diverse types of transportation available in the city of Santo Domingo can assist the foreign visitor to reach his destination from the coastal Malecon Highway where several modern hotels overlook the Caribbean Sea, to the Faro a Colon, the mammoth lighthouse and museum dedicated to Christopher Columbus and the 365 nations of the New World.

However, you may prefer the tropical environment of a mountainous agricultural countryside and farmland for the elimination or prevention of beach boredom. The panoramic and breathtaking view of Cibao, the central section of the nation, was designed to fascinate and infatuate the adventurous tourist and newcomer of the Dominican Republic. Pineapple, platano, yuca, and tobacco farms, rice fields, and orange orchards inhabit the intriguing and incomparable valleys and majestic heights of the central region. The ten thousand foot Pico Duarte and the lesser mountains nearby with their refreshing waterfalls feature a different scenic perspective with every footstep. The foreign traveler may never return to Europe, United States, or Canada with pre-Columbus artifacts during his or her wondrous temporary evasion of urban civilization in the land of Cibao. However, the unforgettable tranquil, benevolent, and hospitable families of Cibao, its cool mountain rivers, and the green hilly terrain and vegetation from Santiago to San Francisco de Marcoris will live in the mind of the visitor forever.

The incredible variety of natural habitat, cultural activities, and Caribbean ethnic traditions flourish in the land Christopher Columbus loved the best. Thousands of North Americans and Europeans are returning year after year to vacation in the sanctuary of variety where beach boredom is rarely a problem.

ARTICLE FOUR

"The Best Warranty In The Caribbean"

"I just got ripped off!" How often have we heard that expression of regret? How often have we said it? The combination of honesty, fairness, and good service is often difficult to find back home in the states anymore.

In North America, fairness means quickness, honesty means read the policy, and good service means your mileage is over the limit. Buy it, take it home, and good luck has become the slogan we live by when we purchase an item.

However; I rediscovered, while living in the Caribbean; honesty, good maintenance, and values that are so often ignored or forgotten in our fast paced city life in the states.

This Caribbean island where I often vacation has an ample supply of shoeshine boys. They are out on the streets early trying to supplement their family's income. They are your first front door salesmen in the city. You'll find them on every corner. They are just outside the stores waiting for your entrance into the streets. In one hand is their shoeshine equipment, and in the other is a large empty milk can that they will use to sit on while shining the public's shoes. They are quick to point out that you'll never make a good impression until you get those shoes cleaned and polished.

I remember one young boy in particular because of his persistence and refusal to accept, "no," for an answer. I was in a hurry to visit as many historical, religious, and cultural landmarks, and other areas of the city. The boy followed me everywhere as he continued his infatuation with my shoes. Every time I stopped to take a picture and to contemplate on what I was viewing, he would point down to my shoes and say, "Your shoes are dirty." This continued for at least an hour.

I decided to submit to the young man's shoeshine rag and black paste after several unsuccessful attempts to get rid of the persistent high-pressure salesman. The five minutes I had during the shoe restoration was spent thinking how I had just been conquered by an eight or nine year old somewhere in the West Indies.

I finally rose from my chair in my shining shoes now ready to give a good impression to the natives of the island. I've learned on this island that clean shoes are an indication that you take pride in yourself and in your work. I gave him the usual fee and tipped him well thinking he'll run back to his buddies and to tell them he landed a big fish.

Man, did I read this kid wrong! He stayed with me into the next street block. I thought, how many times does he wish to triumph over the foreign invasion to his island? I finally stopped, looked down and asked in an angry tone, "Why are you following me again? I paid you double or more for your efforts. I know," he replied, "And that's why I'm still with you. You want more money?" I inquired. "No," he insisted, "I'm waiting for your shoes to get dirty again so I can give you your next shoeshine that you already paid for."

I thought; send this entrepreneur to the states. He'll improve the warranty policy.

ARTICLE FIVE

"Caribbean Honeymoon Rescue"

The last thing I wanted was to be accused of being a kidnapper and end up in jail in my wife's country during our honeymoon. I was forever grateful that I had a little native girl rescue me from my peculiar situation.

The following incident took place in the robust city of Santo Domingo, the capital of the Dominican Republic on the Caribbean island of Hispaniola. We were visiting the family of my wife's brother.

I was taking a brisk walk with my wife's three-year-old niece not far from her parent's house in a very busy sector of the Spanish speaking community. Some of my niece's neighbors already knew that the aunt of this dark-skinned Dominican girl had an English-speaking white gringo husband from the United States. I and my travel companion would soon discover that the news of her newest family member didn't reach into the next street block and beyond.

The lively ebony-colored girl already felt comfortable with my pale skin, blue and green eyes, and a broken Spanish enunciation as we proceeded into "unknown territory" of the city. She was anxious to lead me to the nearest bodega (corner grocery store) for me to purchase her daily sweets.

The little girl finally chose a small family store filled with clients and the sound of the music of Bachata (Dominican country music). Although nobody asked me any questions while I was purchasing her favorite afternoon snack, the curiosity of my presence with a little native girl was apparent in the eyes of everyone. I thanked the owner and we left the bodega in our quest to share our time together as we continued our afternoon walk.

It wasn't long before a man on a small motorcycle abruptly stopped his vehicle in front of me blocking my path. He sharply asked me where I was going with the little girl who now insisted that I hold her. I gently picked up my adopted niece and held her close to me during my conversation with the stranger. Then I politely told him in my poor Spanish that we were just taking a walk on a nice day, and that I didn't need his permission in a free nation.

Unfortunately, that answer didn't satisfy his curiosity. It was not the kind of response that a sociology major should have given to establish a common ground for good international relationships. It only provoked him to continue his "investigation." He even looked around the area as if he wanted a police officer or some other person to assist him in his inquiry.

Prior to asking him in my Spanglish grammar of his interest in our affairs, I realized that this man is doing what I probably would do back home in the United States if the situation was reversed. Here I am in Santo Domingo, a white "gringo" foreigner and stranger in the community walking the streets with a little Dominican girl and speaking broken Spanish with an American accent. Therefore; I concluded, my present confrontation developed only because a citizen was ready to protect his own daughter if necessary. My sociology classes and university degree didn't prepare me for this. I didn't know enough Spanish to explain my presence and relationship with the girl. And even if I did, I doubt if this man would believe me. I also looked around the area for assistance.

Then suddenly the concerned stranger inquired of my niece in his native language, "Who is that white foreign man holding you? Mi tio" (my uncle), she softly answered while compassionately kissing me on the cheek. I responded with a big smile while my opponent looked stupid for the next few minutes.

The man tried to act surprised with the little girl's answer, and in his last attempt to redeem himself, he stated to my wife's niece, "but you're black and he's white."

Young children in any hemisphere know exactly what to say when you have nothing to hide and color of skin isn't an issue. The sweet dark child of my wife's brother just looked into my green and blue eyes and asked, "Uncle, what color are you?"

Not only did I avoid going to prison during my honeymoon, I also learned a new response from a little child in cooling racial tensions. I'm still taking classes in sociology 101, but in a unique kind of university here in the Caribbean.

I walked hand in hand with my new sociology professor as we sought new territory to conquer.

ARTICLE SIX

"Anamuya: The Land Of Green Tranquility"

I would rather visit, vacation, or even live in a habitat that offers environmental variety. For example, in southern California I lived for a short time in a low desert in the city of Indio. I could visit the high desert in one direction in only an hour, or the pine-scented mountains in another direction in less than an hour. The vacation paradise of Punta Cana-Bavaro of eastern Dominican Republic is also near a breath-taking ecological variety.

After three or four days of hot beaches, salty Caribbean water, and the noisy traffic of hotel life, I am ready for a more natural and unspoiled tranquil environment. It exists less than an hour from the hotels in Punta Cana-Bavaro. The area is known as Anamuya. I call it "The Land of Green Tranquility."

There are daily truck safaris to Anamuya from the hotels in Bavaro. Approximately forty minutes from Bavaro is the Higuey Bridge that welcomes you to its city. Do not cross it; instead turn right onto the paved road just before the bridge. The road will eventually lack pavement as it takes you into the roller-coaster hills of Anamuya that is located on the eastern end of the Cordillero Oriental mountain range.

What is so characteristically impressive about Anamuya that hundreds of tourists every year are brought to this area? It offers a tremendous panoramic country relief from an oceanic view just a short distance from the hotels. Anamuya is beauty and tranquility in its own unspoiled environment. I call Anamuya "Green Tranquility" because it is the greenest farming countryside where live the most tranquil families I have ever known in the Dominican Republic.

My first trip to Anamuya was with a native motorcycle taxi driver called a motorconcho. He was also a friend who was working with tourists in the hotels. He knew exactly where to bring me. Here in Anamuya I discovered the peaceful residents of rich farming countryside and high rolling hills sprinkled with the native Dominican Palm Tree. It seemed like the quaint colorful houses of Anamuya constructed near the bottom of the hills were always part of the natural foliage of the green pastures and fields.

The Dominican families of the area are friendly and more than willing to support any effort to welcome fresh conversation and new faces. However; they were a bit shy having their pictures taken. The pale foreign faces of the visiting Europeans and North Americans are now a common sight in the countryside and among the villages of Anamuya.

One of the favorite past-times with the natives during the hot afternoon sun in Anamuya is to cool off in the waters of Rio Sarto de Anamuya flowing through the wooded green valleys. The tourists in the safari excursions are brought by their guides to swim in an open area of the River Sarto that winds along the Anamuya like a giant anaconda.

I highly recommend a safari to "The Land of Green Tranquility" when you are vacationing in the Punta Cana region. You will enjoy the peace with yourself, others, and nature during the precious time spent in Anamuya. Come to vacation in Punta Cana-Bavaro just to visit beautiful and tranquil Anamuya.

ARTICLE SEVEN

"The Stare Of The Children"

Staring at another person is considered rude by many people and even threatening in certain cultures and situations. The so-called "scare" can be a kind of psychological intimidation; especially, when two strangers quietly confront one another. Staring or glaring at others for several minutes at a time has known to instill fear on the recipient. The adult glare from a stranger can be interpreted as a kind of silent plan of bodily attack or mental invasion of the privacy on others by uninvited guests. There is one exception where "the scare" is not meant to be harmful.

The stare of a little child; however, is strictly a result of curiosity and fear. Here in the Dominican Republic I am stared at every day in the streets by young Dominican boys and girls. The little children of this country stare at me almost everywhere. In the streets, bus stations, stores, churches, and in the countryside their little heads will turn in my direction to give me a second look after they have noticed me. I have known children of the Dominican Republic to run in the opposite direction from me after their extended stare and my cautious approach and feeble attempt to speak with them.

I am certain these youthful faces are searching for an explanation when they see something out of the ordinary. I am definitely out of the ordinary in my adopted country. The features of my face, hair, skin color, and language are dramatically different from the majority of the people who live here.

Do my blue and green eyes, partially bald head, and pale skin remind these children of a science fiction movie where white aliens invaded the earth? Maybe that and more! I watch them as they respond to my untimely presence and departure. The human emotions in these children are dramatically obvious. They're mysteriously quiet, curious, afraid, cautious, surprised, and confused.

Some of these little children will immediately ask an adult for an explanation for the stranger's presence and to join them in their curiosity. There are some; however, who will react with affection to a friendly alien. This gentle affection from an innocent child is unavailable in gold and silver or other materialistic charm.

A smile is something we all carry along with us that requires very little interpretation. It all begins in the stare of a child frightened or anxious to be relieved of his curiosity. The stare can be the beginning of friendship and understanding. Wear the smile for our children in our country and you'll return again and again.

ARTICLE EIGHT

"La Machuca"

I can still remember very clearly the hand salute young people of the United States greeted each other during the late 1960's. It was called, "give me some skin." One person would lay open his hand palm upright in front of another individual. The other person would respond by coming down with his palm and drag his hand against the other from near the wrist to the fingertips.

This greeting evolved a few years later into what Americans called, 'give me five;' and then eventually to the 'high five.' The former greeting was used when two persons slapped together each other's hands with arms extended into the air. The later was an addition to the first by jumping into the air while slapping each other's hands at the same time. Give me five and the high five were often seen spontaneously demonstrated in sports after someone had successfully scored or advanced against the opposing team.

Every country needs a good informal and friendly greeting. I was promptly informed that the Dominican Republic is not without its own special, "hello" welcome. I learned by my Dominican co-workers that the modern greeting called, "La Machuca," in the Dominican Republic originated in 1995 when the country's President, Dr. Joaquin Balaguer, began to speak about the easy life in his nation. He said that all things must change and be on a faster pace to keep up with the modern world. Even the traditional handshake was too boring and primitive, and had to be retired. When President Mejia entered office in 2000 he began to greet others with the La Machuca.

The word, 'Machuca,' originally meant to crush or to mash. The fist to fist greeting here in the Dominican Republic will signal to the natives that you are friendly and desire to be accepted as one of the Dominican family. La Machuca has its own effective personality when done with a smile. Not a word has to be spoken when peace and friendliness are displayed through La Machuca.

ARTICLE NINE

"The Unfinished Dream"

The 'dream' of our title is not about the imaging of ideas and events that invade the mind during our evening rest period or in an afternoon nap. It is a person's desire, search, or goal for something more comfortable, suitable, and even pleasurable for oneself and his or her family.

The 'dream' is the ultimate thing that one strives to have in this life. Therefore; one of the most disappointing activities of the mind and hands is the unfinished dream of a human being. It is a tragedy of life! It is a type of human disaster that can literally shorten life by killing the human spirit that seeks to venture beyond the human sight.

The "Unfinished Dream" is visible everyday to all who pass near it in the tranquil countryside and noisy city streets of the Dominican Republic where I live. The sight of an unfinished dream can have one confused, sad, and wondering why it has been left for insects, wandering animals, unwelcome weeds, and human feces.

The unfinished desire of the heart quietly decays in its unburied tomb along busy streets, in urban communities, and country fields. It can become extremely ugly to the viewer and the landscape during the passing years. It may gradually be destroyed by those who are tired of its presence and irrelevant purpose. It is rarely a respected work of the designer and builder. The surviving landlord and his family may avoid visiting or traveling near the site of their failure to complete the unfinished desire of their life's work.

The vacationing foreign visitors to the Dominican Republic will often verbalize their curiosity and confusion of these unfinished fabrications. American tourists often ask me during my transportation excursions with them from the hotels to the airport why the aging concrete skeleton-like buildings they have seen have been left unfinished to helplessly lose their significance in the Caribbean scorching sun. I respond by suggesting that the owners probably had good intentions, but lack the funds or opportunity to finish their life's dream.

Sometimes it is difficult to assume that these deteriorating roadside structures were meant to become houses. Many of them are simply non-connecting walls or solitary corner pillars often embedded during the construction with corroding iron rods that seem like fossilized tentacles frozen in time. The sun-bleached cement pillars that appear to have grown out of the volcanic earth are miniature reminders of the colossal Athenian columns of a lost ancient civilization. Grass, small trees, and other undomesticated Caribbean flora are the unwelcome surviving tenants within the walls of these human tragedies.

Some of these abandoned "dreams" have their four cement block walls, roofs, floors, and plumbing facilities. I lived near one of these undisturbed and unfinished relics. Caribbean vines and other wild green shrubbery now cover the major portion of two walls of the unfortunate house that has been unaltered for years by the mason's cement and the carpenter's hammer. The remaining two walls near the street traffic have been blackened with diesel exhaust, road dust, and the unmerciful elements of nature. The window and door openings of this large and somewhat frightening structure have been partly closed in with plywood and sheets of tin to keep out the curious, the homeless and unwanted trespassers. The unknown darkness within created by desertion, time, and lost of hope is almost a place of horror. It has a haunted house appearance in silent protest to the living while seeking revenge for its uncivilized abandonment and serenity.

Dreams of progress and comfort forever unfinished and unrealized are perhaps more tragic than good intentions to begin a new life. The eroding cement pillars, damaged walls, and other deteriorating structures are now only symbols of determination and effort. Death, economic failure, and lack of opportunity are often life's venomous schemes used in the destruction of hope, tranquility, and the pursuit of happiness and love.

If the desire or dream of your heart is something that you can see and feel with the human touch, it is susceptible to decay and disappointment. It is recorded in the Bible, "Lay not up for yourselves treasures upon the earth, where moth and rust consume, and where thieves break through and steal" (Matthew 6:19 ASV). Fortunately, there is another kind of dream of the human heart that is not subject to physical harm and economical disaster. It is the aspiration of eternal hope. It is the hope that we cannot see with the human eyes or construct with materials of the earth.

ARTICLE TEN

"The Twelve Year Old English Teacher"

The Spanish-speaking Ingrid Fernandez of the mountain city of Bonao in the Dominican Republic came to me after two months as a student in another local English institute. She enlisted in our Easy English Academy paying only a fraction of the fee she had paid previously.

I was privileged to have this talented young lady in our academy. She was far different than the other English students of any age. She had several unique characteristics that did not exist in our other students.

First of all, she had the 'tiger in her eye.' She was hungry to learn the English language. She absorbed everything I taught her. Many others were students in the academy for the social fellowship with their peers, and for being distinguished as foreign language students of their community.

Ingrid would finish between four to eight pages of English studies per class hour. She never failed to ask for homework over the weekend. The weekend was a time of play and rest for the others who were less motivated.

There was another trait that made the pleasant smiling Ingrid special, and separated her from the other students. She had a goal for her life even at the tender age of twelve. She wanted to establish her own English school here in the Dominican Republic. Her dream made me a little nervous. She would be the best competition I would have in the city. I would make her the director of the Easy English Academy as soon as she was able to fulfill the position.

The third characteristic that made her special is that she insisted on teaching younger children what she already learned. Ingrid understood that learning by doing, or on the job training as we call it in the states, was an academic process that would enhance her English skills. At the age of twelve, she became my youngest English teacher.

This remarkable Caribbean girl completed her study book and the first level of English in one month that normally takes other students three months to complete.

Ingrid still has what it takes to succeed in life. She has the desirability to achieve and a worthwhile purpose for her life. Besides these personal qualities, Ingrid Fernandez believes in helping others to succeed. Ingrid doesn't know it yet, but she is already a member of the future teaching staff of the Easy English Academy.

ARTICLE ELEVEN

"Where Creativity Is Original"

I abhor copycats; those who plagiarize the ideas of others and claim to be the authors and owners of the product.

I have always admired cultural originality and creativity. Perhaps these two rare jewels will not have to be chiseled from stone. They already exist! They are free in the open market of this country. Originality and creativity are often born when and where there is not the possibility and the opportunity to copy.

Children from economically-depressed communities are some of the original inventors. What they cannot buy, they imagine that it can exist in another form. Crude creativity and originality are necessities when financial resources are not available. I have discovered these two jewels in the Caribbean only two hours by plane from the Miami International Airport.

The Dominican Republic is the home of many well-known major-league baseball players. Sammy Sosa is perhaps the most famous Dominican slugger during the writing of this article. There are not many Americans who are as fortunate as me. I have traveled through the hometown of Sosa many times. I have seen and used some of the original baseball equipment used by Sosa and other players.

I have also witnessed creativity from the minds of children and the building of original toys. Old mops and broom sticks no longer useful for cleaning were perhaps the original baseball bats that Juan Marichual and Sammy Sosa used as young boys playing on the city "ballpark" streets or in the countryside near the sugarcane fields. Sammy's first "hard balls" thrown to him were probably large discarded plastic caps of five gallon water bottles that are presently used by Dominican youngsters. Perhaps one day I will be remembered as helping to develop a future baseball slugger or home-run hitter when I was pitching bottle caps for him to hit on the streets while living in the Dominican Republic.

The creative children of this nation will find a way to replace the real things with items that adults consider trash. These happy young people are clever inventors, and are never being credited for developing some of the original toys.

For example, Dominican slingshots are made out of large rubber bands and small y-shaped guayaba tree sticks or can holders. A small waterless coconut and a clothes line with hanging string along the line will be used as volleyball equipment. Stilts are made out of large empty cooking oil cans attached by twine to produce the forward movements of the person standing on the cans. Open plastic bags, cut light sticks, and string are the ingredients used for making kites that often can be seen flying several hundred yards above the city buildings during the windy months of March and April. Large empty cooking oil cans, used bicycle and automobile tires are pushed with sticks by children along the streets while running as fast as they can. Short wide wooden sticks smaller on one end are used as tennis rackets. A double AA battery and a string can be made into a spinning battery 'top.' Try it; it works! Baseballs are made from old socks rolled and tied together by a piece of string.

I live amidst all of this creativity in the warm climate of the Dominican Republic. My daughter and grandchildren were born here. There're Dominican and imaginative persons. Here comes one now. He's holding in his hand the bottom part of a luggage bag used by tourists. This section of the bag has four small plastic wheels. They're attached to a metal plate that is glued to the bag's bottom portion. I watched him as he cut two sets of wheels from the discarded luggage bag. Two skate boards were carved from the street garbage. No blueprints were used! I just saved $50 bucks!

ARTICLE TWELVE

"The Bodega"

The Bodega is one of the most fascinating places in the Caribbean to visit from eight to eleven in the morning. The three hour daily period of cultural unrehearsed entertainment is one of the greatest contributions to human freedom and diversity.

The owners of "The Bodega" avoid charging admission. It's free enjoyment for children and adults seven days a week. The Bodega should become a frequent scheduled tourist attraction. I have no knowledge of any excursion or tour that visits the Bodega at the present time.

I've convinced my native wife that I should be making daily visits to the nearby Bodega in order to understand more fully the Latin-American Dominican society in which I am living. This morning is no different. It's a ritual now. She hands me a piece of paper with a list of Spanish words and instructions that must be read aloud and repeated several times to the staff of the Bodega.

It's nearly eleven o'clock when I leave my house to become a participant at one of my favorite cultural centers. I'm late today. I fear that I have missed most of the conversation and activity, and that the audience and actors have already returned to their residences. My daily appearance is expected. I'll not disappoint the familiar faces that patronize the Bodega.

I'm now within sight of the community's favorite expressive association. Its doors are still open. The Bodega never closes during business hours. Besides, there is always a constant flow of human traffic going in and out of the Bodega. Today there are several one-man motorcycles called passolas in front of the two small doors leading into the one-room congested building. There is also a table and four chairs already positioned in front of the entrance for the very elderly who need to sit. I'm in luck! People from the community are still entering. Perhaps there is also a special event that has captured the interest of those who normally go elsewhere.

I have finally arrived and a familiar aroma permeates the atmosphere. There is barely enough space to squeeze between the patrons of this popular tiny crowded establishment. The majority at the Bodega are women who are constantly trying to get the attention of the staff. My partially bald-head and white skin Caucasian features are easily spotted by the audience and the employees.

I thought I heard my name being used by the owner, Chico, who is behind his fading white plywood counter. Before I can even greet anyone, I am interrupted by one of the locals standing near the owner. "Ask the American. He just arrived," he shouts out as everyone turns and looks in my direction. Ask me what? I pondered to myself.

"How do you say chuletas and pollo in English?" questioned a young woman curious enough to learn a few foreign words. "Pork chops and chicken," I enthusiastically answered. "Gracias," she responded. "How do you say cebollas in English," another woman in the crowd questioned while the owner approaches her with his large kitchen knife. "Onions," I quickly answered. "Are there any more ques................" Wham! The sharp heavy blade slams into a bloody carving board interrupting my response and severing a leg from the wet dead body with its slimy skin and fat exposed to the menacing flies.

The customers nearest the table counter have now slightly backed away from the unfortunate victim as Chico again demonstrates his unusual talent. Wham! Wham! Another leg is severed and the chest is split apart. "If you can't stand the sacrificial blood, you may want to leave," the owner kindly informs newcomers like me. I pretend that I didn't hear him.

"Twenty-five pesos a pound? Yesterday it was twenty-two pesos! Last week it was twenty! And tomorrow it will probably be thirty pesos! I can't believe this!" exclaims a boisterous and disappointed woman. "Mateo, (my name in the Dominican Republic) this doesn't happen in New York, does it?" questioned one of the younger women who slowly walks toward the exit with a fresh young victim in a plastic bag.

They're all looking at me now as if they need some emotional relief from their economic disappointment in life.

"I don't know, but I'm sure it does. I've never lived in New York. I'm a country boy from a small town in Oklahoma," I gracefully admitted.

"The American, he's going home one day, and we'll still be here. He has a bodega back in New York where the prices don't go up," explains one of the more philosophical attendees. "Si, Mateo, you're here now at our bodega, but tomorrow you'll be in yours where the prices don't go up," another voice comments to my misinterpreted and misunderstood American lifestyle.

Now I'm beginning to feel like a foreigner and an outsider at the bodega today. They've labeled me and pushed me into a particular minority class that has status in this country. I don't think I like it. I feel like a stranger when they do this. I can't change my appearance and my American accent. I will always look and speak like an American. Regardless, how do I become different in order that I am looked upon as one of them? Give me another thirty years at the Bodega and it might happen.

I pulled out the tiny piece of paper that my wife had given me for this occasion. I read the instructions that were written in Spanish. "Give me two sopitas, one sazon liquido, and two pounds of rice," I enthusiastically yell out in Spanish to the owner's beautiful young wife. Having the loudest voice among the present clients, I promptly receive my request.

I'm once again discovered when a new arrival enters the Bodega while quietly inching my way to the exit with my package of purchased items. "Are you an American?" the large Dominican man asks me in English. "Yes," I timidly respond. "Wait a minute. You speak my language. Who are you?" I ask with excitement in my voice.

"I am your friend. God bless America, the stars and stripes forever," he screams to the top of his voice. Now I want to run out of here, I'm thinking. "I love the United States. I'll fight anyone who puts a hand on you!" he adds with a friendly smile on his face.

"Do you always come here in the morning?" I inquire as I would to my long lost brother. "No, actually I have been purchasing my food in another bodega, but not anymore if this is where you come. I'm here today to get the latest news and gossip from these people, and.......and to find a new friend, like you! An American, finally, at the bodega and living in my city," he responds with a loud voice while gripping my hand.

We said our good-byes with a future expectation of another encounter. "American apple pie gringo, see you tomorrow, I hope," he shouts as he walks in the opposite direction proudly portraying the American flag on his shirt. Wow! I made a friend at the Bodega who is more American than an American!

I arrived at my house at least an hour later than I should have. I handed over the simple food and spice items to my wife with a mischievous grin on my face. She only asked one question. "Honey, what happened at the Bodega? You're late and you look exhausted."

"What happened at the Bodega?" I repeated with excitement in my voice. "Well, another chicken was slaughtered. Look at the blood on my shirt! Twenty-five pesos a pound! The people are really upset. I was in a questionnaire contest to see if I understood Spanish. They accused me of living in New York again and having my own Bodega. The people don't believe prices go up in the states. I made an instant friendship of a Dominican who is more of an American than I. Then I was publicly embarrassed when the people of the Bodega gave me an importance above others," I finally concluded.

"Oh, great, just another normal day again at the Bodega," my wife responded. "Maybe you can find another colmado (family grocery store) that has a little more conversational variety for you," she concluded as I quietly retreated to the bedroom for privacy. Now I know why there are no organized tourist tours to the Bodega.

ARTICLE THIRTEEN

"My Country's Flag Is No Stranger"

America never looks so good when you live outside of her. An American living as a foreigner appreciates more of his country's freedom, learns to sing his national anthem, and teaches his native language.

The American living abroad sees everywhere the human quest to live and to be a part of the best.....United States of America.

When I arrived in the Caribbean in the summer of 1999, I was told more than once that I was the boss. Well, I thought, if I was the chief, where were my Indians? I finally inquired why I was considered "the boss" living as a foreigner. "You're an American," the natives explained. "You're a part of the best and everything we want. Most of us here want to live and work where you came from." I looked around where I was standing and I understood.

"I want to go to America!" can be seen expressed on envious faces everywhere in this land. T-shirts, underwear, caps, jeans, toys, and even umbrellas are often decorated with my country's flag. I've never seen the flag of Castro's Cuba or Chavez's Venezuela, for example, on any form of material worn by the people in my adopted tropical country.

Recently I enjoyed listening to a song sung in Spanish that was very popular here titled, "America." The song described the Hemisphere of the Americas as a beautiful garden. Most people; however, were thinking about the United States whenever they heard the song. The people of this gorgeous tranquil island seem convinced that the United States of America is the garden where they prefer to live and cultivate. The American Consulate in this nation's capital is busy processing thousands of applications for those waiting to live as Americans.

America is not everything in life, but the world desires what she has. There is crime on the streets of America, but criminals are looked upon as the destroyers of our civilization. The American government has a heart for those who are naked and deprived of bread. Our government protects the liberal and the traditionalist for their opinions and pursuit of values. Not everyone lives in America, but the world wants in.

America! Your name brings hope to the stranger
And pride to your sons and daughters
Who live far off in other lands.
Your Constitution is the classic document of government.
It Works!
What a shame to lose what we have.

America is not perfect, but she is precious! Those who drift on rafts, yolas, and other floatable material from foreign countries to our shores will give their lives to taste the preciousness of our freedom and way of life. Many of these hungry pilgrims will guard America's ancient truths and protect her way of life far better than many of our citizens.

America, America, the melting pot and the garden spot of the world looks more beautiful to me now that I live with so much less. I am hesitant to criticize and condemn America when she represents hope and life to a destitute world longing for an opportunity.

My country's flag is no stranger! I see it everywhere here in this tropical paradise. The people wear my flag, not burn it!

ARTICLE FOURTEEN

"Caribbean's Holy Birds"

My West Indies wife and I decided to return and live in her native Caribbean island for the remaining of our lives. I knew there would be some surprises and changes in many of my living habits, but I was willing to take the chance and learn to adapt to the new environment.

What I desired the most in life for our family were security, happiness, and a loving environment. I decided I would first listen and learn about these important ingredients of life in my new country.

I'm a religious man so I decided I would go to church while in the capital city and pray about this. I can also get acquainted with some of the local people. I thought, what could be so different from the states in going to church except for the Language (Spanish) and some of the customs and traditions? I'm sure I will find peace of mind.

It was very hot during church services. The small congregation had a large ceiling fan to cool the members. I looked up to see why the fan was not sending out a breath of cool air in our direction. Well, the fan was turning, but no one was receiving any air except for three baby birds. They were nestled among grass and sticks on the inside cover of the fan peacefully waiting for the return of their mother.

Then suddenly and without warning the mother bird swiftly flew into the church building above the preacher's head while grasping an insect in its mouth for her little nestlings. The bird calmly flew inside the fan just below the dangerous rotating blades while the minister was spiritually feeding his family. His sermon was titled, "Eating the Bread of Life." What an ironical contrast display of life, I thought. A bird and a minister were doing similar work and in the same building.

I was sitting at a perfect position to view the coming in and the going out of the mother bird. The enthusiastic creature made five trips in and out of the church house during the entire service. Each time the bird had food in its mouth for her youngsters. It appeared that the minister had a resident member who took to heart his lesson on feeding the hungry and lost. Holy bird!

Nothing seemed to disturb the contented feathered settlers living just below danger and death. Surprisingly, they had everything a family needed. How clever of the mother bird to build it's nest in a church fan where there were security, the proper temperature, and a shelter surrounded by a loving environment. I surmised, that's exactly what I want for my family.

While we were all singing the closing hymn of the service, "I'll Fly Away," the obedient bird made a quick brief flight above the congregation and out of the church as if to say, "I love this one!"

"I really like going to church a lot here in the Dominican Republic. The sermon gets illustrated right in front of you by nature herself," I remarked to my wife during our trip home. I also apologized to my wife that I didn't remember much about the minister's sermon. I was constantly being "distracted" by another minister feeding her feathered flock.

Perhaps I can also learn to adapt to my new unfamiliar circumstances. A family of birds found security, happiness, and a loving environment near one of the most dangerous places-a rotating blade on a small ceiling fan. I learned something today. I also found peace for my soul. I will not be afraid to live here. Next week I'll return to the same lively church for more bird lessons on survival in a foreign land. Holy Birds!

Article Fifteen

"Paradise Untold"

I eventually forgot the reason I am barely surviving and eating the unseasoned and tasteless food of country peasants and street beggars. I never knew the hardships of life that robbed the soul of dignity and hope until I was immersed in these doleful circumstances infused by an exaggerated persuasion to live in Paradise Untold.

I don't believe there is an earthly paradise; only in the hungering desire for something new to quench the spirit of its dryness. Perhaps we look for extremes to provide us happiness. Perhaps I discovered all of the extremes only to find a world of discomfort oblivious to personal gratification.

I migrated to the Central Cordillera Mountain Range of this Caribbean island many summers ago before the turn of the century when I was still economically independent from the native inhabitants. Perhaps out of sheer boredom of living, the lack of strong family relationships, and cultural conflicts in my native society were sufficient reasons to convince me to live in my discovered Paradise.

I could no longer emotionally live and adjust to changes in the new millennia's modern society of the urban and small town life of the United States. I was looking for societal interrelationships and daily communication with neighbors and townspeople similar to my small native coastal Maine community. I was searching for spontaneous communicable freedom that existed in the past. I was seeking for what most Americans have lost in their communities-a friendly response.

It troubled me that I could not bring the past into the future. There were radio stations in Oklahoma playing old rock songs from the fifties and sixties. I lived in that period of time again when the Beetles sang, "Yesterday." But I could not find a society in America where neighbors vigorously and daily speak to one another outside the doors of their houses. I'm a man of history, I concluded. I'm an outdated person. I wish for something that brings harmony to the soul and to a community. It doesn't exist anymore in our "fast-paced close the door and leave me alone" culture. Television and the Internet are the new ambassadors of congeniality.

I will never forget walking alone each day on the deserted dusty streets of my former western Oklahoma prairie town near the Red River. I met no one in my quest for fellowship and conversation. I would briefly pause at every fifth or sixth house anxiously desiring for the resident within to exist from his front door. A dog would often appear to chase me away from his territory if I got too close. I did not dare to walk in the direction of a house if there was a small child playing in his or her yard. Strangers and children together can create controversy. I avoided that.

What happened to sociality in America? People don't talk anymore on the streets. Modern air conditioning and malls have replaced streets. I became frustrated with my country's new behavior. I exiled from boredom and emptiness in my quest for paradise and the past.

I lived comfortably three and a half years here in the Dominican Republic as a tourist guide for American and Canadian tourists during the winter months. Summer arrived and things changed economically. There was no work and my savings was eaten up from daily expenses. I have recently learned to eat rice, beans, platanos (green cooked bananas), and yuca (a native root) since I had no tip money from the tourists to purchase the food that I prefer to eat.

White-collar work for foreigners such as myself is nonexistent in the valley of the Yuna and Blanco Rivers where I now live. However; life in the mountains is simpler and cheaper. Here I've also discovered variety in the environment and an hourly exchange of viewpoints. I inherited more of the past than I bargained for.

What I call, "territorial neighbors," are encircled in our street in plastic chairs playing dominoes and gossiping about the recent habitual power loss in our city. Haitian women, followed by their young children, are balancing baskets of clothes on their heads while peddling their goods from house to house trying to make a sale. An older man carrying a greasy bucket is selling pigskin meat. Several ice-cream carts roll along our street every afternoon while the owners ring their tiny bells in hopes of tempting hot thirsty residents. A buyer and seller of gold and jewelry announces his intentions on his portable loudspeaker. Pickups with huge loud speakers larger than refrigerators are blasting out business advertisements or the coming of local festivals. A native farmer from the mountainous countryside pushes a crude wooden cart selling avocados, lettuce, and other green vegetables. A small Toyota pickup is burdened down with green bananas, yuca, and eggs.

Several young people with long wooden sticks and large plastic bottle caps are engaged in their daily play of baseball. Crowds of twenty or more people have quickly rushed to the scene of a neighborhood brawl of street fighting between two adults. Adolescents with baseball bats down the street are chasing a thief caught in the act of stealing. A neighbor robbed by the thief fires in the air a round from his pistol.

Several neighbors seeking relief from the hot rays of the sun have now stationed their activities under a large tree in front of my rented house. A preacher on his motorcycle equipped with an auto battery and two speakers preaches as he slowly maneuvers his mobile pulpit down our community avenue. Our neighbor's naked baby makes his morning appearance at our iron-barred door.

There's never a dull moment in this society. I am never given a moment's peace. "Quiet! Leave me alone," can often be heard from my living room where I am trying to write my next book. But they never leave you alone. Here in the past they never leave you alone. No one here believes in privacy, I concluded. A variety of menaces have become my new disappointment with life. Oklahoma was never like this. How peaceful and relaxing it was to be there. I can't believe I said that!

I've developed a new habit. Every morning I vigorously stare up at the peaceful tropical green mountains silently and gallantly portraying their dominance over our city below. I'm wondering if life there is friendlier and more tranquil. Is there a paradise where the Yuna and Blanco Rivers harmoniously mate nearly five thousand feet above the hot noisy valley? I can't stand the suspense of not investigating the unknown. The human soul feeds on another point of view in its quest for contentment and survival. There is the possibility of a paradise waiting for me near the clouds and above the pain and uncertain life of this city.

One week later I found a fresh breath of natural freedom and social life along the Yuna River forty minutes above the city. There is a community of a dozen or more aging cement and wooden houses just before the bridge that crosses the swift Yuna River. It's so peaceful here! Is this Paradise, finally? I contemplated.

My new mountain river society for now is safe, friendly, and sociable. The happy and inquisitive children always seek my whereabouts to learn a few more English words. The community's only family grocery store seems to have an early afternoon "happy hour" when everyone is invited to share and hear the latest news and gossip. This is my community newspaper, I thought.

One of my mountain neighbor families has constructed near the bank of the river a crude stone stove for cooking, and a small wooden shelter that is attached to their house for the selling of cooked green bananas, pigskins, and deserts.

Bathing is easy near the clouds. The cool river water is uncontaminated and full of large eatable crayfish. Here there is instant refreshment for my aging flesh and bones during the hot afternoons. Below the large cement bottom of the bridge is where the women gather to clean themselves while washing their clothes in the Yuna. Occasionally a minibus will cross over our bridge carrying tourists to the river's reservoir twenty more minutes up into the mountain wilderness. A huge crowd from the city of the valley will gather along the river during a fiesta weekend.

During each afternoon around four o'clock I drift on my stomach like a dead carcass in a tranquil pool in the cool clear river while staring at crayfish on the bottom searching for safety from my alien eyes and threatening hands. Without exception each sweet-water crab locates a sandy crevice and squeezes into its tiny natural rocky pocket. Has an animal that rarely visits the surface and smells the colorful flowers near its habitat discovered its

41

paradise? I wondered as the bulging peevish eyes of the crustacean follows my movements in the water.

Tonight is peaceful and it's too early to retire for the evening. I am looking for an electrical outlet to plug in my computer to resume writing my book. Where is it? There isn't one! What, no electricity? Progress has not yet arrived on the mountain. The valley has electricity. The city below was never like this. How refreshing it was to be near the breeze of an electric fan while working with my computer in the valley. I can't believe I said that!

I will retire early. No computer and television! Nothing electrical for miles! Wait a minute! No noise! No molestation! Privacy finally! I think I like that. What am I complaining about? This is what I have been searching for all my life; a tranquil location with a friendly environment. I will go to sleep without a revenge for my society. Paradise finally!

The Yuna River reflected the friendly light of the moon for the first few hours of sleep. It began to rain just before midnight. The wet dark atmosphere and the nearby river were perfect conditions for the night feeding of mosquitoes. They had no trouble finding my tanned white skin and its supply of fresh warm blood. I was already bitten a dozen times or more before I succeeded in placing the mosquito net over my bed. I felt safe and comfortable again. Paradise was waiting to give its newest resident a good night sleep.

Suddenly the moon completely vanished from sight. Dark ugly clouds gathered for their nightly display of anger. The word, "anger," is a gentle description for the vicious presence of thunder and lightning that invaded our mountain this evening.

It rained and rained. It was raining harder than I had ever witnessed in my life. I couldn't help but think about the biblical story of Noah and his ark. The noise of the rain drops on my tin roof sounded like the simultaneous pounding of several hundred hammers. This continued for several hours. I never went back to sleep.

Finally at daybreak I heard a new sound from the river. It was the sound of water, but a lot of water. I opened the rear door to witness a river that had gone mad. The quiet little pools of water that were used for bathing were all gone. It was now dangerous to even wade there. The raging river rose several feet above its normal height. The bank of the river near our settlement was disintegrating like ice in a glass of hot water. The rolling gushes of water that hit huge boulders in the river would often spit out from its watery graveyard pieces of broken wood beams with tin used on the roof of houses.

I see several people gathered near my house. They are speaking about the two homes that have already been washed away in the night. They've also concluded that it's too dangerous to be staying in this area. Many families will have to move out of their houses. The fragile plywood and tin will soon disappear in the unforgiving swift current of the Yuna. I will go with them down into the city of the valley.

Some of my neighbors refuse to go down into a city of strangers to be stared upon while waiting near the streets for the end of the crisis. They chose instead to move to higher ground as far away from danger as possible. I despised the adolescent behavior of the city people, and I also wanted to climb up along the mountainside and wait there for the end of the storm. But I would not be able due to the injuries to my lower back and an ankle. The majority of the village people prepared to go into the city below on their small motorcycles. The remainder went with me in my old jeep. Oklahoma was never like this! I can't believe I said that!

The journey to the city of the valley is slow and cautious. Several storm streams that are crossing the pavement from higher ground are now breaking apart the road tar. The angry river on my left is an uncomfortable close distance from our vehicle.

"Look out up ahead," yelled one of the front seat passengers. But it was too late. "Bang!" The noise I feared the most at this moment. I ran into a large menacing road hole filled with dirty water from the storm. The tire of the left wheel blew apart as it slammed into a sharp edge of the deep hole due to the speed and weight of the vehicle.

"What are we going to do now? It is too far and dangerous to walk to the city below," exclaimed one of the fearful adult women from the village. "Where are we?" I asked as I slipped out into the rain and wind from the security and dryness of the crippled vehicle. Nature did the rest. The wind, rain, and blackness of that hour gradually swept us downward into the valley of regret.

Six months later I moved back into the southeastern province of my adopted country resuming my work as a tourist guide. On September 16th of the same year (2004) Hurricane Jeanne ripped the roof off my rented house and left me homeless with seventeen thousand others in our city.

I soon moved to Utah looking for work and the quiet life of the states. Instead, I was plagued with boredom once again that left me critical of the present American culture. I can't believe I said that!

Here I'm just another small fish in a large pond. Paradise is where I was needed! I was never bored there. See you soon, Dominican Republic.

ARTICLE SIXTEEN

"The Sierras Of The Caribbean"

Santo Domingo, the capital city of the Dominican Republic, offers almost everything one would find in a large city of the United States. Hundreds of thousands live here due to economic and social necessity. However; there are those who seek refuge and peace of mind daily from the hot cement jungle of the Caribbean metropolis. There is a national haven for those who cherish tranquility and friendliness, and resist the hectic and noisy life of the large cities. These migratory pilgrims look toward Cibao.

Very few tourists who vacation in the Dominican Republic rarely visit and view one of the most beautiful and spectacular regions of this island. Majestic and mountainous Cibao is the cure from the scorching sun, the salty sea, and the tourist noise of hotels for foreign adventurers and curious vacationers seeking variety of nature, culture, and recreational areas.

MOUNTAIN PARADISE

Cibao or the central region of the country acts like a magnet pulling you into its fertile bosom and surrounding you with its embryonic country hills and mountainous terrain. You will soon discover the arrival in another world when leaving the busy and congested capital city of Santo Domingo and traveling north on Highway One that goes all the way to the Atlantic coastal city of Monte Cristi.

All of a sudden and without warning, an incredible invisible scenic door opens. Towering mountain peaks, sloping hills, and green valleys begin the conspiracy of a love affair with the mind. Paradise invites you to its domain.

Everywhere in Cibao can be seen sunny fertile valleys laden with various kinds of crops. Cibao is the bread basket of the Dominican Republic. Its rich agricultural soil produces almost everything from coffee and tobacco products, rice, beans, various kinds of vegetables, bananas, citrus fruits such as oranges and pineapples, lechosa and chinola (passion fruit). Cibao is also the national home of milk and cheese products. Many farmers also raise chickens, pigs, cattle, goats, and much more. The large Dominican cities and the dozens of hotels along the coconut palm beaches will depend daily on being supplied with fresh food from the Cibaon countryside.

Quite visible from many major roads can be seen some of Cibao's hills and mountain peaks that are partly stripped of its trees and other natural greenery by the mining and production of the nation's gold, silver, nickel, and other minerals and metals. There are also beer and rum distilleries, chemical factories, textile mills, and the production of materials used for construction.

Last but not least, Cibao is also the birthplace of some of the most beautiful and compassionate young women of the Caribbean. Cibao may also be the last known frontier and paradise of love for those of us over fifty.

However; the casual highway traveler and viewer will never see the immeasurable depth of Cibao's beauty until a trip is made up on the challenging panoramic roads near the rivers of the mountain canyons. I recommend stopping in the city of Bonao on Route One and ask for the mountain road leading up to the Yuna and Blanco Rivers.

The Sierras of the Caribbean known as Cordillera Central Massif has the highest elevation in the country and the lowest temperatures. The temperatures in the area near the city of Constanza and Mount Pico Duarte have known to drop as low as thirty-two degrees Fahrenheit in January.

The crystal-clear icy waters of the high central mountain rivers eagerly forfeit their place of birth among the clouds on the rapid voyage to the valley floor. These mesmerizing streams help give life to the rice fields and other crops and vegetation on their way to the sea.

The voice of these rivers rippling over layers of rocks lying beneath its wet blanket echoes its presence and preeminence in the cool mountain evening air. There are many areas in these enchanting rivers where the currents are dangerously swift during the rainy season and wading across the other side would be impossible. However; the river bed hiker will not find it impossible to walk up many of these tropical rivers during the dry season. Small fish, fresh water shrimp, and spiny crayfish flourish in these streams. Colorful plants and flowers of various species occupy the wet rocky lagoons near the river's edge.

Winding rugged roads and trails along the rivers will assist in bringing the curious visitor closer to Cibao's colorful majestic views. A different perspective of the countryside can be seen on each curve in the roads. These paramount pine-scented mountains such as Pico Duarte, the highest peak and king of the Caribbean Sierras, will not annoy the temptation to stare for hours at the panoramic magnificence. Therefore; one cannot resist in going further up and deeper into seclusion of the Cibao. A variety of scenic activities await the aggressive adventurer.

High altitude fields that have been cleared for grazing and growing crops are sprinkled among the dense forested hills. The luscious green fields appear to be at a vertical level with the horizon when looking straight up from the base of a canyon or valley. Cattle can be seen feeding like mountain goats near the top of these slopes.

Cacao fruit, or the basic ingredient used for making chocolate, can be found growing along trails and sharing the same soil with the green banana plants. The bread fruit trees with its fruit resembling in taste like bread are growing on slanted banks near the trails and small dirt roads.

The falling of cool sweet water from the rocky cliffs sends out an inviting wet spray to the thirsty traveler who happens to walk near its revered ground. Many enchanted waterfalls can be found among the mountains of Cibao. Small old one or two-room wooden shanties with their tin roofs hiding among the mountainous forest vegetation give shelter to the few who desire freedom and seclusion from the noisy and painful life in the valleys below. The rows of palm trees that grow near the clouds on the mountains of Cibao are reminders that the land is tropical and part of the Caribbean experience.

April, May, and November in the Dominican Republic are rainy months that bring relief to the dry thirsty land of the Cibao. I have witnessed some of the most spectacular display of cloud activity in the valleys of this region during the rainy season. Thick white foamy clouds on the wet mountainous peaks appear to be mammoth-like arms and hands of snow smothering the life beneath. Slowly the puffs of cotton-colored froth empty its mist into the early morning valleys.

When the moonlit night falls into the area, human romance will seek its height. The moon over Cibao in the late evening offers a sensational exhibit of its influence against the splendid alpine regions. The moon's beacons of light seem to burn right through the evening's darkest clouds. It also appears that one can almost reach up and put his or her hand around the bright ball of the night and bring it down to the earth.

THE MYSTERY OF CIBAO

Cibao is much more than mountains, unspoiled green valleys, canyons, and rivers. It is more than a place to view and vacation. The land offers life and hope for the future to those who are patient and faithful dwellers. Cibao is a way of life that supersedes survival. There is a mystery to this country that touches the human soul. If you are one of the few strangers who seek a route from the capital city to the north Atlantic shore, you must pass through this great land. When you do, Cibao will claim you for its own; and you will return to love it again and again.

The Dominican families that live on the rural mountainous hills and in the valleys of small cities and towns of Cibao understand the hope and peace that their land inspires and produces. They remain in Cibao knowing there is more serenity in this land than anywhere beyond. The overall experience of Cibao territory and its way of life has drawn me into its existence. I am no longer considered a pilgrim. I am also Cibao!

ARTICLE SEVENTEEN

"quisqueya Cuisine Of The Dominican Republic"

The original Taino Indians of Hispaniola (today Haiti and the Dominican Republic share the same island) called the island, Quisqueya, or Bohio. Quisqueya is a native Indian word of the Dominican Republic meaning, "Mother of all lands." Christopher Columbus called the island La Española on December 9, 1492, four days after discovering the Caribbean tropical paradise for Spain. It was the land he loved the most, and it was here that he asked to be buried.

THE CARIBBEAN DIET

Can a person really eat the food he or she enjoys while on vacation abroad in the Dominican Republic and still lose weight? Yes, I did, and I didn't even count the calories.

It was easy for me to forget about trying to eat the same kind of food from back home while living in my adopted Dominican environment. I learned to enjoy the rich culture and the abundant delicious non-canned foods while losing pounds of fat in my first two weeks in this country.

How did I lose those ten ugly pounds of lazy fat without trying hard? Did I carry with me a notebook with the instructions of a strict diet? Did I spend hours in front of an expensive hypnotist? Was I running ten miles a day along the beaches while my friends were having fun in the water?

No, none of these things were part of my life. However; I selectively consumed everything sitting in front of me. I also did the following things that rebelled against my American fast-pace lifestyle:

1. I ate plenty of the natural and unprocessed meats, fruits, and vegetables. There were very few occasions to eat any canned and processed foods. Perhaps you are visiting a Dominican family on the island. I suggest that you eat the food that needs to be cooked with that family instead of purchasing it on the streets. The Dominican woman of the

house will know if the food is fresh and how long it needs to be cooked. Here is a list of some of the food that I gradually accepted as part of my Dominican Republic diet:

Locrio-a decilious meal of rice and meat (chicken, pork chops, beef).
Moro-beans cooked together with rice.
Mondongo-a soup of tripe (cow´s stomach) with vegetables.
Cosido-a soup of pata de vaca (cow´s feet).
Asopao-moist rice with meat or fish.
Bacalao-cod fish and potatoes or rice.
Rabo de vaca-soup with meat of the cow´s (hairless) tail.
Chivo gisado-goat meat cooked in its own sauce.
Crab in coconut sauce-a cooked meal of fish or crab with coconut.
Sancocho-a delicious thick seasoned soup stuffed with beef, pork, chicken, goat, fish, vegetables, and roots (ñame and yuca).
Cazabe-unleavened yucca bread. I love it with peanut butter.
longaniza-a long spicy sausage that has been hanging in the Caribbean sun all day.
Chicharrones-pig´s skins with pieces of lime.
Also fish, platanos (plantains), rice, beans, various fruits, and fruit juices such as orange, pineapple, chinola, tamarindo, lechosa, and granadilla.
Mangos, pineapples, coconuts, sugar cane can be found everywhere to be eaten for an afternoon natural snack.

2. I substituted all the soft drinks with water and natural juices.
3. I daily drank 8-10 large glasses of water.
4. I walked three to four times as much as I did back in the United States while getting acquainted with the natives. This was not a vigorous chore since it was a pleasant part of my work.
5. I couldn't find any junk food and buffets to eat.
6. I did some physical survival work that had to be done in replace of the modern conveniences I used to have in the United States, such as carrying bathing water into the house.
7. I avoided eating a heavy meal late in the evening.
8. I went to bed slightly hungry almost every night.

I hate to ruin your day, but I am now fifteen pounds lighter and two inches smaller in the waste and have more energy to do the things I enjoy. I am spoiled living here in the Dominican Republic without many of the modern conveniences. I'm afraid to return to my home country for an easier life. It will make me fat again. However, I welcome you to join me. Get healthier while you´re having fun. It's not against the law. It's the Caribbean diet!

Article Eighteen

"Scattered Seeds"

Sometimes a random and thoughtless act can have good and productive results. What we do with the results should be our greatest concern so it will profit the many or the one.

I was cleaning out the mushy "guts" and the seeds of a small Caribbean orange squash that my wife would use in the preparation of the cooking of red beans. I gathered up the uneatable vegetarian "intestines" of the squash and thoughtlessly threw them out of the open wooden door of our house in the back yard that bordered a small polluted community stream. It appeared that the unwanted seeds "safely" landed in the southeast section of my fenced-in weedy virgin garden under a coconut palm tree and near two young lechosa plants.

I hadn't committed a crime by discarding something that would soon decompose into the ground under the scorching Caribbean sun. I didn't go to bed that evening speculating about the seeds of the squash scattered behind my house. I didn't lose a second of sleep thinking how cruel I had been to something that only birds would probably ingest. I soon forgot about my random act.

Each day I walked passed the tiny garden several times thinking nothing about my thoughtless act. Nine or ten days later the neighbors who live in the small tilting tin and wooden house bordering our lot mentioned that something different was happening on my land under the coconut tree. "Come and see," they insisted.

They were right! There were two thick green vines coming out of the ground and growing in opposite directions. Each vine had five or six large green leaves growing from it. Could it be vines from the seeds that were not even purposefully planted into the soil of the ground? I decided to wait a few more weeks before I passed judgment and my machete on the mysterious uninvited vegetarian growth.

In one month's time the discarded tiny black seeds of a Caribbean soup and bean squash had sprouted twenty-foot vines twisting and turning on anything that happened to be in their way. A few weeks later the thick green vegetarian "snakes" had completely covered the yard and were seeking other terrain and objects for their affection.

The only disappointment I had with the law of nature and my thoughtlessness was the absence of space for my late afternoon yard chair. Where will I place it so as to enjoy the early evening rats eating the day's table garbage near the trickling brook, and the childhood antics of my neighbor's small daughter?

My machete and I hesitated to remove our new green ground resident that enthusiastically grows without my personal attention. There are now so many question I have concerning my new vine invader that appears to be sterile. Does it have a right to exist? Will it eventually produce the soup squash that I love so much? After all, it lives and continues to grow from discarded seeds of an orange bean squash. I have no right to take its life! It has stimulated my interest in the nature of this beautiful country.

ARTICLE NINETEEN

Dominican Recipes

"CESO-EGG COOKED FRUIT"

Ceso is a natural fruit from a fifteen to twenty-foot tree found in the Caribbean islands. Many of the inhabitants of the Dominican Republic will be the fortunate owners of a ceso fruit tree.

Ingredients you will need the following to feed 4-6 persons:

1. Two dozen hand-picked ceso fruit
2. Four eggs
3. One Spanish onion
4. One section of garlic
5. One sopita
6. Sazon liquido
7. Vegetable oil

Instructions
1. Select and hand pick two dozen clusters of the ceso fruit from its tree.
2. Remove the fruit from its protective covering or peeling. There will normally be three sections of the ceso fruit in each"ball" or cluster.
3. Remove and discard the large black seed that will be located in the middle of the ceso fruit. Also remove and discard all of the red skin that may be around and inside the fruit. The black seed will split the ceso fruit into two halves. Each half can be opened easily with a spoon where the red skin may be "hiding"
4. Boil two quarts of water in a pot.
5. Place all the ceso fruit in the boiling water and cook until the fruit is very soft.
6. Remove all of the water from the cooked fruit and mash the cooked ceso with a fork.

7. Mix together four eggs, one sliced Spanish onion, one mashed section of garlic, one sopìta, and one tablespoon of sazon liquido.

8. Put one teaspoon of vegetable oil in a small frying pan.

9. Place the mixed seasonings in the frying pan. Stir-fry and cook for only one minute.

10. Mix the mashed cooked ceso fruit together with the stirred-fried seasonings.

11. Serve the delicious ceso cooked fruit in small bowls. It has a taste only found in the West Indies.

Ceso fruit is also delicious when it is cooked with cod fish. It may be served as an appetizer, desert, or with the main meal.

ARTICLE TWENTY

Chinese- Caribbean Seasoned Chicken
(Pollo al carbon)

INGREDIENTS: You will need the following to feed 4-6 persons:

One whole chicken
One bottle of Chinese sauce or salt of mota
One garlic ball
One green pepper
One Spanish onion
Oregano

INSTRUCTIONS:
1. Slice one garlic ball.
2. Slice into small pieces one green pepper.
3. Slice into small pieces one Spanish onion.
4. You need one tablespoon of oregano.
5. Ground together the garlic, green pepper, onion, and oregano.
6. Mix three tablespoons of Chinese sauce together with the ground ingredients and set them aside for the moment.
7. Poke holes in the entire body of the chicken.
8. Place the chicken in a sauce pan five or six inches deep.
9. Pour the ingredients over the entire body of the chicken.
10. Cover the pan and cook the chicken in the oven at 325 degrees for two hours.
11. Check the meat of the chicken at the end of the two hours to be sure that it is cooked to your liking. Leave the chicken in the oven longer if necessary. The best texture for taste is when the meat can be easily removed from the bone.
12. Serve the entire chicken in its sauce. Delicious!

Warning! If you serve this recipe to your neighbors, you may never have a day of peace. They'll try to find excuses to be invited to dinner again and again hoping for the same dish.

ARTICLE TWENTY-ONE

"Caribbean Stuffed Peppers"

INGREDIENTS: you will need the following to feed 4-6 persons:

Six large green (red, yellow) peppers.
One pound of white rice
One pound of ground beef
One Spanish onion
One garlic ball
One sopita cube
Liquid Spanish sazon.

INSTRUCTIONS:
1. Cook one pound of rice for 30 minutes.
2. Boil one pot of water four inches deep with the sopita cube until boiling.
3. Carefully cut it large enough so you can remove the seeds from the inside. Be sure not to damage or throw away the section you will remove. Later you will use it to seal in the meat and rice.
4. When the rice is finished cooking, mix the raw ground beef together with the cooked rice.
5. Cut up the onion and garlic into small pieces.
6. Mix the onions and garlic together with the rice and ground beef.
7. Stuff the rice and meat mixture into the stuff peppers.
8. Put one tablespoon of the liquid Spanish sazon on the ground beef and rice mixture while it is in the pepper.
9. Seal the seasoned peppers with the cut-off tops.
8. Carefully place upright the stuffed peppers into the seasoned hot water.
9. Slowly boil the seasoned water until the peppers and beef are cooked. Add more water if the level of the boiling water drops two inches below the top of the peppers.

10. Gently take the top off each pepper to see if the ground beef is still soft but has been thoroughly cooked.
11. Serve the delicious Caribbean stuffed peppers with potatoes or other non green vegetables.

Comments: The sopita and the liquid Spanish sazon can usually be purchased in the ethnic section of a large supermarket.

ARTICLE TWENTY-TWO

Crab In Coconut Sauce
(CANGREJO EN COCO)
Providencia Matthews

Caribbean fresh water crabs can be found in most large inland lagoons located near the ocean. Many of these large crabs in the West Indies will leave their moist underground holes during and after a heavy rain. Many of the crabs will be caught by the natives on the country roads near the lagoons during the rain.

INGREDIENTS: You will need the following to feed 4-6 persons:

12 crabs
One can of carnation milk or cream of coconut
Bottle of lemon juice or 4 lemons
One Spanish onion
One cilatro leaf
One section of garlic
One green pepper
One small can of tomato paste
Salt

INSTRUCTIONS:
1. Cut the crabs in chunks or large pieces.
2. Cut off and throw away the scale section just below the neck.
3. Wash thoroughly the crabs with the lemons or lemon juice.
4. Add and stir one can of can milk or cream of coconut with each 12 crabs in a pot by themselves. Set the crabs and cream of coconut aside.
5. Cut in small pieces one onion.
6. Cut in pieces a small section of cilantro.
7. Mash one tablespoon of garlic.

8. Cut in small pieces one green pepper.

9. Add three tablespoons of tomato paste to the ingredients.

10. Also add two tablespoons of salt to the ingredients.

11. Put all the ingredients, except the crabs, together in a large pot.

12. Add three cups of water to the ingredients.

13. Boil the ingredients for 10 minutes.

14. Place the coconut crabs into the boiled or cooked ingredients.

15. Boil everything together for 15 minutes.

16. Stir continually the crabs and the sauce while boiling.

17. Add more salt if needed for your taste.

18. Serve the crabs and its sauce in a platter. Delicious!

It will be very difficult to find a crab delicacy as good as this recipe. Serve this dish to your very best friends. They'll be there when you need them.

ARTICLE TWENTY-THREE

"An American Man "

"Mira! You, the American man!
Visit our streets if you can,
Eat our food, drink our beer,
Dance to Merengue music here."

I'm an American man, they say,
Sometimes lost in the crowd,
It's not long before I'm found,
For I wear the face of An American Man,
My clothes, my speech, my food, my hair.

I fear that my name will never be heard,
Only Mr. American Man.
Call me White, anglo, or a Gringo?
I'm a foreigner in my own land,
For they always see me as An American Man.

Will I be found? Will I be heard,
Above ancient history and a sterile song,
"An American Man."
Even in church I will hear,
"Will you stand and give us your name,
American Man."

An American Man with blue and green eyes,
That's all I am to cultural spies.
And during each day, as often as I can
I live in my closet away from the band

that plays the same old melody,
"The American Man."

I can't take it any longer,
Cultural suspicion and emotional pain,
Day after day, it's all the same,
"American Man, do you have a name?"

Now ask all the little children
On any street where I've been,
It's not the American,
It's not the Gringo man.

It's "Mateo, Mateo, Mateo come here!"
They run with excitement
They jump into my arms
They touch a warm tear
Before it falls to the ground.

Their kisses on my neck,
Their gentle whispers of love,
Reminds a divided world
Don't see me as a color.

Listen to the children repeat
In any language so sweet,
And I know you'll understand some day,
As they sing a song, a new way.

"American Man, you have no color,
No language that frightens me,
Mateo, I love you more than what I see."

Listen to the Dominican children if you can
Visit the family culture to understand,
A life that takes your heart and soul
Though not by force, by love alone!

ARTICLE TWENTY-FOUR

"The Mysterious Caves Of Veron"

The road south from the "sunrise" cities of Higuey and La Otra Banda eventually finds its way into the growing town of Veron where the majority of its residents work with the local tourist industry. Restless Veron (**or Beron**) connects the scenic vacationing communities of Bavaro and Punta Cana with its present new development of highways. Just a few miles north from the crossroads where the roads of Bavaro and Punta Cana converge in Veron survives an unannounced village trail for those who choose to inhabit the priceless solitude of country woods and fields.

A four-wheel drive vehicle, an off-the-road motorcycle, or a mule would be the necessary forms of transportation for the twenty to thirty minute rugged rustic excursion to the mysterious sinkhole "Indian" caves of Veron.

I found at least three of these tranquil dark caves totally hidden at ground level from the eyes of humans. All of them have several feet of cool fresh water inhabited by a species of blind fish. Like the underground dwellings discovered in other locations in the Dominican Republic, it is possible that the pacific Taino Indians or the more hostile and warlike Caribs who came up from South America lived in these remote caves situated about five miles from the waters of the Canal de la Mona. At the present there is no proof that these three caves were the homes of these ancient Indian people.

The Taino Indians, the people who welcomed Christopher Columbus on his arrival, are believed to have originated from Central and South America. The word Taíno meant 'good' or 'noble' in their language. These are the Indians who showed Columbus and his Spanish crew their peaceful and generous hospitality. Recent estimates indicate there were probably several million Taíno living on the island at this time. When Columbus crossed the Atlantic with his crew of Spaniards, he made stops on what is now known as the islands of the Bahamas and Cuba before landing on the island he named Hispaniola. The Taínos called the island, Quisqueya, Haití, or Bohío. It was here in Hispaniola that the Spaniards got excited for several reasons. Columbus' journal is full of descriptions indicating how beautiful the island paradise was, including high, forested mountains and large river valleys.

He described the Taíno as very peaceful, generous and cooperative with the Europeans, and as a result, the Europeans saw the Taíno as easy targets to conquer. In addition, they saw the Taíno had gold ornaments and jewelry from the deposits of gold found in Hispaniola's rivers. So after a month or so of feasting and exploring the northern coast of Hispaniola, Columbus hurried back to Spain to announce his successful discovery - but he had lost his flagship and had to leave many of his crewmen behind.

Did the Tainos eventually find security and safety from the Europeans in these secluded and peaceful underground cave fortresses in the countryside surrounding Veron, Bavaro, and Punta Cana? Were the island Indians living in them even prior to Columbus' discovery of Hispaniola? Perhaps the tourists and other visitors to this island will discover the answers to these questions when they crawl into the unwritten past that seems to permeate the mysterious caves of Veron.

ARTICLE TWENTY-FIVE

"Twenty-one Reasons To Spend Your Vacation In The Dominican Republic"

1. See the original baseball equipment of slugger Sammy Sosa in every town-used mop or broom sticks for bats, and large plastic bottle caps for baseballs.

2. Ride with 24 other people in the back of a small Toyota pickup truck.

3. Cut and eat your own sugar cane in its field along the highways while the nearby Haitian men harvest the crop.

4. Asked to be kissed by a passing beautiful young native woman without being slapped and accused of being a male chauvinist.

5. Hear 10 different native songs on the same street from 10 different consecutive stores.

6. Drive down the wrong way of a one-way street while a national police officer may be casually looking the other way.

7. Watch a winter snowstorm in New England on a television while relaxing near a swimming pool with sunburn sipping a pineapple colada.

8. Date two beautiful women on the same date.

9. Get married to a person half your age.

10. Eat pollo al carbon (oven-seasoned chicken) and yuca in a restaurant all night in the capital city of Santo Domingo.

11. Dance on the street by yourself to a Merengue or Bachata tune without being accused of being crazy.

12. Block one side of the street with a table and chairs while playing dominoes with your friends.

13. Speak with children of the same family whom all may differ in color from one another.

14. Ride with a motorcycle taxi for less than fifty cents (20 pesos).

15. Hear a sermon being preached by a passenger on a public bus while en-route to its destination.

16. Be caught up in an atmosphere that will inspire a new honeymoon with your spouse.

17. Cash in one American dollar for about 32 pesos.

18. Visit the highest and most beautiful mountains of any Caribbean island (The highest is over 10,000 feet).

19. Hear a musical concert at a car wash.

20. Walk with the spirits of the Spanish conquerors into the oldest buildings in the New World.

21. Enjoy more freedom than you've ever had in your life.

Author Robert Matthews and his wife, Providencia

www.ingramcontent.com/pod-product-compliance
Lightning Source LLC
Chambersburg PA
CBHW052010280526
45793CB00005B/921